PALM

incorporating 'A Day in T'

and with a Foreword by Ca   ..umens

2002. 坂12

Also by David Cobb:

A Leap in the Light, Equinox, 1991 (0-9517103-0-3)

Mounting Shadows, Equinox, 1992 (0-9517103-1-1)
　　　(Haiku Society of America Merit Book Award, 1992)

Jumping from Kiyomizu, Iron Press, 1996 (0-906228-56-5)
　　　(Haiku Society of America Merit Book Award, 1997)

The Spring Journey to the Saxon Shore, Equinox, 1997 (0-9517103-3-8)
　　　(Woodnotes (California) Haibun Award, 1996)

A Bowl of Sloes, Snapshot Press, 2000 (0-9526773-3-4)

The British Museum Haiku, British Museum Press, 2002 (0-7141240-1-X)

The Dead Poets' Cabaret, Iron Press, due 2003

David Cobb was born and raised a few miles north of London, where both urban and rural life were at the door. That his childhood was being blighted by the Great Depression, he was then unaware: 'moral rearmament', Bible classes, the Blitz and fast bowling were more obvious hazards to enjoyment of life. Youth was dominated by nearly four years of national service (trooper, Household Cavalry armoured car regiment, duties connected with occupation and peace-keeping) during which he saw Germany, Egypt, Palestine; aged twenty-five he made it almost unexpectedly to university (Bristol), where he read German. Anticipating a working life as a grammar school teacher, he found providence taking him in other directions: with Unesco to Hamburg; with the British Council to Bangkok; eventually, on the staff of an international publishing house, to many other countries in Europe, the Middle East, and Africa, as an author and adviser in the field of English as a foreign or second language. He came to haiku while observing Japanese schools in 1977, but did not publish any poetry until 1989. Since 1985 a freelance writer, he lives in a village in East Anglia. Before retiring from the game in 2001 he calculates he played in about twelve hundred cricket matches.

Cobb's wish is that haiku and haibun should find a secure (if properly modest) niche in English literature – literature celebrating life as it comes and capable of invigorating our times – and if he has been at all impetuous in this attempt, he might resort to Ezra Pound's defence: 'error is all in the not done, all in the diffidence that faltered'.

David Cobb

PALM

Equinox Press

This edition published in the UK by Equinox Press
Sinodun   Shalford   Essex CM7 5HN

ISBN 0 9517103 4 6
British Library Cataloguing in Publication Data
A catalogue record for the book is available from
the British Library

First published 2002
© David Cobb, 2002
© Foreword Carol Rumens, 2002

Linocut and handprint by the author; crayon portrait by Georgie Roy
Printed and bound in Great Britain by
Biddles Ltd, Guildford and King's Lynn

Acknowledgements I wish to thank these editors who first gave recognition to some of this work: John Barlow, in Snapshot Press publications; Peter Mortimer, in Iron Press publications; Michael Mackmin, in *The Rialto;* Colin Blundell, in Hub Editions; Jackie Hardy, Caroline Gourlay and Colin Blundell again, in *Blithe Spirit;* Randy Brooks, in *Mayfly;* Wim Lofvers, in *Woodpecker;* Martin Lucas and Fred Schofield in *Presence;* Kevin Bailey, in *HQ;* Graham Ackroyd, in *Nineties Poetry;* Michael Dylan Welch, in *Tundra* and *Wedge of Light;* Ban'ya Natsuishi, in *Ginyu;* Jim Norton, in *Haiku Spirit;* Lee Gurga, in *Modern Haiku;* Jim Kacian, in *American Haibun and Haiga;* Alec Finlay, in *Football Haiku;* and Jean George and Michael McClintock in *Journeys.* I owe a particular debt to Carol Rumens, Ken Jones, Graham High, Mimi Khalvati and Claire Bugler Hewitt for saving me from a good deal of batter on my face; and to Kathleen Basford, Charlotte Bernays Smith, Barbara Sachs Clark, Meriel Lland, Marianne Kiauta, Janet Blundell, Louis and Julia Alexander, Nigel Jenkins (where does one stop!) for encouraging me to go on tossing up the pancakes anyway.

contents

foreword

David Cobb's haiku are unusually three-dimensional examples of a form that often seems, in English at least, somewhat flat. As the delightful compound titles of his haiku sets and sequences suggest (*codpoppies, sinslap, whistlesmile*, for example), Cobb is a writer who enjoys making connections and crossing borders. The traditional distinction between haiku (concerned with the 'natural' world) and senryu (human-centred and mostly humorous) scarcely seems to operate in his work. Characteristically, he is alert to ingenious combinations of the two:

> polling day –
> swallows swooping
> through a mist of flies

Perhaps it's because the relish for minor incident and local, every-day detail is so evenly balanced and closely interwoven with the response to the elemental and timeless that a haiku by Cobb seems much larger than its tiny scale. As in a good short story, the reader is invited 'to see a world in a grain of sand.'

Haiku technique is often compared to photography. But why should a modern writer limit himself to snapshots? Here, there are sets and sequences that flash and glimmer and change focus like intriguing short movies. Cinema, David Mamet has said, 'shows us what the light was like.' A reel of haiku by Cobb can show us exactly what the light was like, and how it changed. And the work engages with our other senses. It may evoke the smell, the taste, the sensation on the fingertips –

> snow on the sill
> the prisoner's finger
> sneaking through the bars

– or the sounds in our ears:

> a bee enters
>   its buzz
>   in the foxglove

The stereophonic master-stroke here, 'its buzz', reminds us how important a resource assonance is to haiku. As for metaphor and simile, the art is to juxtapose images, and let the reader's imagination do the rest:

whelks all over the beach auntie's bunions

There are no taboos in Cobb's work: sex, war, bodily functions and urban squalor coexist with nightingales and moonlight. The haiku form is treated as a fully functioning vehicle for the contemporary sensibility, and not as a walled garden to which connoisseurs only are invited.

Besides a rich variety of haiku sets and sequences, *Palm* contains haibun (haiku + prose), translations of work by several classical Chinese authors, and original longer poems. The writer's slant on the world remains wry and individual: moments of transformation are drawn from a lightly teased, but cherished quotidian, whatever the medium. 'Please respect the dust', the last line of a poem called 'Dust Care', might be an epigraph for the whole collection.

Readers will be stimulated by *Palm* to question received suspicions that techniques of writing haiku and 'straight' poetry are somehow essentially different. Distillation is the raison d'etre of both, after all, and Cobb's work demonstrates that a good poem in seventeen lines will be just as focused and economical as a poem in seventeen (or fewer) syllables.

The following pages will certainly delight haiku afficionados, but their appeal is much wider, and should reach lovers of good writing in all genres. Those who have not so far enjoyed haiku will surely be pleasantly surprised. Whether or not this *Palm* contains infinity, it certainly holds out a generous scoopful of wise, touching, darkly gentle poetry that reveals more of its essence at each re-reading.

Carol Rumens

nettlebuzz

a bee enters
     its buzz
          in the foxglove

cool white concrete
stretching out   the shade-
bathing cat

          a tortoiseshell
             follows the winding
      brook
          nettle

        by nettle

wine in my hand
mullein caterpillars
     fat with sleep

cuckooscent

                         nothing of June –
                 only the cold stiff kneebones
                 of inaudible bees

from afar, a cuckoo
    cracks in the lawn
      pull apart

            clouds race
            the poppies'
            shortest night

all through the darkness
within their own scent
night-scented stocks

tidesmell and cockledog

        a shift in the wind –
thistledown starts to blow
in from the sea

                the brown retriever
          abandoning dog smells
          for the smell of ocean

whelks all over the beach auntie's bunions

        on-shore breeze
        on my leg wet-cold
        the spaniel's lick

another tide
the beached whale's jawbone
      deeper in the sand

          a moment between
          lighthouse flashes
              cold smell of fish

boats left to winter
clacking of frozen halyards
against sheetless masts

preserve pot

This preserve pot of cherrywood
with its tight cherrywood lid
tight as a pip in an unripe
nectarine and its hole not an ant
could squeeze through past the spoon
to this day never had jam in it.
I bought it the morning after
we had composed ourselves
and now it is quite full up with
things I never use:
keys for unrecognised
padlocks, a small curl of hair,
a dead man's worry beads
and a ring with a ruby too like
the Renaissance for me now to wear.

dust care

Would you please see that my door
is off the latch, in the porch trim down
your larger feelings, before you step in
in your stockinged feet perhaps:
I may not be observing protocol myself, or
dressed for visitors, and certainly not
armed to resist an intruder.
I would resent a spring
cleaning or even a mild
tidying up. Even if known to me
please announce yourself. I am where
sometimes in untidy surroundings
two can meet without fuss.
Please respect the dust.

at a cemetery on Epiphany Way

In Berlin on a late summer's day the Epiphanienweg leads to a cemetery called Luisenfriedhof. I am coming to see you, Corporal Gabler. My second visit. After fifty years.

Monuments face each other across the gravel path, so that the acute morning sun, creating a serried pattern of shadows, strikes the blank rears of those on my left, whilst lighting up the inscribed faces of those on my right.

The place is full of flowers and German widows. The widows stare at me, they tend graves, some of them recording loved ones born in the very year you died. Almost-old-comrade in the enemy army, on the last day of the war you stepped into the street, wearing your civvies, at the command of a Russian patrol, and outside your home you were shot through the head. And now it's my duty to bring you news of your widow, that she too is lying at peace, though in some corner of an English field.

Weren't we all three confirmed Romantics? The triangle has to be closed.

The sun is very warm today and, traversing row after row of tombstones, I can't find you anywhere. As I speak to you, *Wo steckst du denn?*, I wonder if it's in order to call you *du*. We were never properly introduced, we never even spoke. Just I stood beside her at the grave, holding a trowel that was out of shape, while she laid flowers on you. That day, also in summer.

Rest, we all wished you rest, thinking of *ewige Ruh'*. But now, fifty years on, when I ask the gardener with a watering can in his hand where you might be concealed, he shakes his head, tells me – and I know he means help – to ask at the office. A plot for *Gabler?* Maybe his tenure ...?

> 'Rest in Peace' –
> and just nearby a plaque,
> 'Lease expired.'

I cannot face the office, go to the Lietzenseepark instead, where 'the public are requested to respect the local residents' need of repose.' A Turkish family are spreading out a picnic, a Chinese woman goes through the unhurried postures of Tai-Chi, weeping willows touch the surface of the lake.

It is still beautiful, the bombing had not stopped the tulips, do you remember, *Liebchen?* I think of sitting down in Babylon and weeping, and in that moment a faint shower begins.

> a sound I can't hear
> the consciousness of leaves
> receiving rain ...

Tanabata sash *(a sequence)*

kodō drumming
       an indistinct path
       through *bonsai* trees

                small weeds
                – they have tasted earthquakes
                    and the chop of hoes

a flash, hot rain
big-spotting the pavements
fragrant dust

                Ginza shopping
                stunted gargoyles
                of umbrella spokes

in all lengths of hair
it blows itself out
the summer storm

                torpid heat
                a housefly too confused
                to leave the train

as much as they can
on a leaf too small for them
       two butterflies

                lovers on a bridge
                straddling the plash
                of golden carp

                              ripe fruit
                              in a paper bag
                              storm rain

at the old wooden inn
a basin and a tap
for two to share

                              fixing his robe
                              her fingers simplify
                              the starched blue sash

for her secret diary
oranges rolling wet
on the rushmat floor

                              paper walls
                              partitions for small hours
                              when women shriek

he stretches at last
into the Chinese character
for greatness ...

                              from the glow of flares
                              snatching silver fish
                              black cormorants

in a darker wind
hands in each other's pockets
rhododendron leaves

sunslip

eclipse of the sun
a snail slides out
from under a stone

                barbecue
                hairs on the cook's belly
                sprinkled with salt

harbour wall
sand slips from the mark
of the record tide

                sun coming out
                now on the seventh day
                her two-week tattoo

          into the waves
        moonlight scuttles away
      on the backs of crabs

                towards sunset
                the riptide rolling
                an empty crabshell

slim hands peel oranges

Slim hands peel oranges to tempt her lover,
she plies a knife with still-as-water sheen,
it comes from Bing-Chou surely as the salt
that's snowed upon the fruit was mined at Wu.

A reed pipe on her lips she places,
offers a wooden flute and lifts her eyes,
the warming notes disperse into the haze
of censers, bronze, and curtains of brocade.

"Do you give thought where you will take your lodging?
The watchman on the walls has signalled three
times with his rattle, and the frost's like tin-tacks.
It might be just as well ... you spend the night?"

after the Chinese of Chou Pang-yen

not one bird

Not one bird on a thousand hills,
Snow without footprints on ten thousand paths,
yet, in sedge hat and straw jacket, a fisherman
cracks the ice and starts to bait a hook.

after the Chinese of Liu Chung-yuen

worm lick

      wormdiggers' mittens
e x t e n d i n g f i n g e r n a i l s
     towards mugs of tea

                stepping stones

                in the middle of next stride
                a wasp at rest

before I have time
to ask what breed it is
the Dobermann's lick

                rain   at last
                in the neighbours' front yard
                    the yacht gets wet

plastic pond
a frog jumps
past it

cockroach

We're company, this night of repetitions;
through a bathroom door, ajar,
I watch distractedly your
revision of the bathmat –
do you swot for some examination
on body juices of my migrant fellows,
who wrestling with the threadless tap
at various times impregnated their sweat
from souring toenails into your pabulum,
and then took showers, if the water ran?

You cock your querulous antennae
in my direction on the unmade bed,
where I, supine and naked, semi-read
my novel of some African intrigue.
Agents we are, no doubt of rival powers,
aliased, and informed by different codes,
obliged to hole up in the same safe-house
until this storms runs out. And all the while,
static has clogged our pores – confess, you
perspire under your folded wings?

And when it comes, the power cut, as it must,
you with your mandibles continue chewing:
your comforter is edible in gloom.
Not so my novel, though it smells of dripping.
This is the end, chum, of our concordat,
I'm vowing never more to take this stink,
share it with you, after the lights come on.
Till then, as you chew, suck, chew,
and slobber on your victuals, bear in mind,
I in the dark revolt to hear you eat.

bednest

An Essex river washes the last specks of African soil from between the toes of martins as they pick up mud from its shallows. They have come back to the nest made last year and the year before that, intent on remaking it. They copulate under Venus, roost under the Milky Way.

> unfledged chicks
> clamour in the eaves
> their first full moon

The martins' nest is cemented in the window angle of the spare bedroom, the one where I retreat when I have a bad cough. In May we prepare for them with care, setting the window ajar and leaving it, whatever the weather, so that the parent birds aren't scared away from feeding their young, or disturbed in their scant hours of huddled rest. Before the window may be shut again it is opaque with droppings. Guano piles on the sill. Once in ten years the house decorator chips it onto the peony below.

> new coat of paint
> not even the martins' nest
> can hold it back

Now it is the fledgelings' heads coming out of the slit entrance to cheep for food, next their rumps voiding globules of an almost pure white shit.

> o Moon,
> your petticoat trailing –
> in that splodge of lime!

A dead chick has never been cast out of the nest, not once in twenty years. This cheers me as I lie in my narrow bed beneath it.

> ill in the dark
> a twitter from inside
> the martins' nest

resolution

Hills to the north and south are thick with graves
and at Ching Ming the living jostle too,
carrying gifts to their ancestors.
Like butterflies the joss-paper ashes fly,
azaleas drip, and little children weep;
but after sunset the burial mounds
are once more foxes' dens.
                    Now, going home,
children laugh in the lantern-lights.
I shall get drunk tonight, and every night
long as I shall live, for now I'm sure
there'll not be one drop of good liquor
in the After World!

after the Chinese of Kso Jui-shiuan

happy hour

The pull, the rounded arm,
the gleaming brass, the spill
of beer on knotted timber bar:
"Your usual?" she asks,
and draws my evening pint.
We watch the froth rise slowly up the jar.

And then, my "Join me too?" disclaimed
with one switched impulse of a curling brow,
we start to talk of children, near and far.
The curtains, like our separate days,
are pulled unhurriedly to lap.
We watch the froth sink slowly down the jar.

the school Christmas show

Six-thirty. December evening. Raw weather whisps in from the playground, follows parents through the double doors of the primary school hall.

> a child blows
> into a balloon
> the balloon blows back

Grown-ups slacken scarves, reduce themselves onto chairs designed for tots, suppress seasonal coughs and sneezes as the head teacher haw-hums for attention. Some announcements. Draws a monitory finger out of his trousers pocket to point to a bucket. Hopes no child will feel sick again like last year, but ... Please look out also for the Class Six children stationed by the door when leaving. They'll be holding out basins. The collection this year is for those with Alzheimer's.

> trapped on a girder
> above the *Exit* sign
> a shuttlecock

Parents pointing out their favourite bits in the handmade programme. "Isn't that a lovely drawing my Dot's done of Santa Claus?" Like a figure made with matchsticks stuck into a potato. Class One will be first on stage.

> tiniest girl in school
> holds
> up
>
> the star

Mrs Cavendish lifts the piano lid, removes a toffee paper from middle C and begins to play *The First Nowell.* A small child with a fringe and rouged cheeks climbs onto the makeshift stage and says we're in the fields near Beffliam. The fields creak as the flock plods in, one of the shepherds sneezes over a sheep, one of the sheep waves to his mum.

nativity play
red face of the angel
coming on too soon

Later, things are made better for the tearful angel. When Mary gets into difficulties extracting the baby from the folds of her dress, the angel helps the ox to deliver the immaculate birth.

Joseph takes the Jesus doll from Mary's lap and plonks it in a cardboard box, one of the Wise Men reflects that it may suffocate under the straw and uncovers its face. Mrs Ogilvy prompts another of the Wise Men, in a clarion whisper, "Go on, say something to the baby!"

The Wise Man peers intently at the Jesus and says, "You've got your father's eyes."

Joseph, shepherds, angels, Wise Men, the ass, the ox, the sheep, assemble under the spell of Mrs Cavendish's baton and sing *Away in a Manger*. Mary turns her toes in and keeps her thoughts to herself.

And outside again.

blurred walls
glimpses through the mist
of fairy lights

family carols

We feel our way along the dark path to the village church, each step insecure of its landing, eyes on the belfry, where shadows of ringers are cast by a naked bulb through the unglazed openings that people used to call the 'dream holes'. The peal has two notes missing, the change is never complete, but tonight of all nights this is not heard as a blemish.

        the churchyard sloshy
            suddenly underfoot
                a grave that's firm

   Mother, well on into her eighties, has my arm around her waist.
Hoisted, so her feet barely scrape the ground, I notice her weight is so little
now; I feel I shall never hold her again like this; I am carrying almost a ghost.
   She is borne to where we are as close to the crib as we can get, leans
on me in the pew, gazes milkily at the Christmas tree, gaudily bedecked with
baubles, tinsel, but as yet unlit.
   The focus of our good nature becomes the vicar, an 'ancient and
modern' sort of man. Warning us now, when we set light to our candles, not
to ignite the coat-tails of someone in front. Has provided a pail of water by
the pulpit, just in case. The verger has a towel, but hopes there'll be no one
this year for an early bath. Encourages us to chuckle with him at his annual
joke.
   My mother's face expressionless the while, until the organ pipes
croon out hoarsely the first familiar tune. *While shepherds watched ...*

            a song she knows well
            on the back of my hand
            warm drops of wax

   Now she has a halo of animation around her lapsed cheeks, she has
transformed into a Victorian schoolgirl again, singing for farthings on a
doorstep. Singing her favourite, and just in time. When we sit down at the
end of it, she snoozes against my shoulder without snoring.

            soft touch of leather
            my bewildered mother's
            worn-out purse

   As we leave through the porch she slips a small coin into the vicar's
hand and wishes him "Happy Easter!"

snowstains

                                    frost holds
                            Friesians in the byre
                            chew steam

snow lingers on
in one right-angle
of the wayside cross

                            on the fixture list
                            the name of the groundsman
                            we buried last week

                            day of his funeral
                                    still inviting messages
                            'after the tone'

            sunlight fading
    through the stained glass windows
            laid-up flags

                            throughout the sermon
                            pondering the question
                            why do snails climb walls?

at the Rec

> dark side of the fence
> white shadow
> of the frost

    Onlookers huddle by the end where they hope the goals will come, shuffle in their wet wellies and press leaves deeper into the mud. From time to time, through the fog, the wraith of a greasy football, shouts of "Pass! Pass! Pass!" A heavier thud, it hits the goal net and carries on through a gap in the mesh. One of the spectators, stiff in the legs, goes off to fetch it from a bush, wipes off the dog-slime that has stuck to it.

    Gloved hands, muffled clapping, a thin cheer.

> touchline
> the spat catarrh
> of ageing men

moon flash

sparrow
            held in my hand
its eye   a ruin of blood
         planning escape

air raid
      in each bomb flash
the magenta eyes
     of cats on heat

after the all-clear
remembering nothing
but the kiss

the moon half-full
she pencils her eyebrows
rounder still

onion glint

on glinting tiles
the pigeon's strut
prints on the frost

Paganini
sun
on icicles

stillest of days
the growth of onions
out of onion bags

on each newlaid egg
a blue flake
of henhouse paint

ladder pedals

old walking shoes
fitting like new
camellias bursting

                    at the spring fair
                  the wind   freeing
                              free balloons

a cloudless sky
painters stretch ladders
      to their furthest rungs ...

                tiles missing
             through the rafters
                      swifts ...

corduroy jeans
so long since I had them on
      my knees whistle

            pedalling uphill
               I am overtaken
          by a butterfly

codpoppies (a sequence)

Wednesday market
dribble freezes
on the jaws of cod

> the smell of onions
> in the mackerels' eyes

at the quick-serve till
checked out with each item
her engagement ring

> the change she slips to me
> chill in my groin

couple aged eighty
carrying a dozen eggs
between them

> a long argument
> about the sell-by date

two minutes' silence
we stop swinging
our red shopping bags

> no pencil
> my poem goes to Ladbrokes
> to be jotted down

daffodil morning

on the misty pear
all of a sudden buds
burst into sparrows

blackthorn in bloom
I drive a full mile
       with lights undipped

                behind the coal box
                a black cat licks the wind
                out of its fur

daffodil morning –
      looking for something
           very blue to wear

                    wouldn't you swear
                plumb centre of each raindrop
                there is blackbird song?

      equinox:
above closed celandines
    the stars come out

                clocks going forward
                the foetus six months old
                thrusts out a foot

rendezvous

Beneath the shingle bank, not quite out of the wind, a sunny spot. Sitting on a drying path through the saltmarsh, at last I pull a shirt on over my vest as the sun goes in.

Eight small figures rise above the shingle bank horizon like an awaited dawn. At legionary pace they advance, silhouettes with the wind behind them, but for a long time the crunch of their boots is not blown towards me.

Relieved to find I took the right decision about where to wait for them. In the village my enquiries had me sent off, not on one wrong track, but three different ones. To get the last of these misdirections I had to buy a pint.

> "Up thish alley, shir ..."
> my guide with hay-fever
> and hands to his nose

Half an hour later the map tells me the path I'm walking today is the one I should be walking tomorrow. I'm on the western bank of a small estuary when I ought to be on the eastern one. But I see two young women wading across, water up to where calves begin to nip in to knees, and I surely won't be out of my depth if I follow them.

"Come on, it's quite safe," one calls out to me, thinking I hesitate.

"I know, I saw your legs," I reply oafishly. And then, after I've slithered my feet through silt and sand, she offers me a tissue to wipe them clean.

The women tell me they're staying in Stiffkey and I think to repay their solicitude by telling them about the one-time rector there. The story of Willy Davidson and the beast. How among London's red lights he recruited girls to sing in his church choir. Defrocked for this, earned a living by preaching sermons to a lion in a menagerie cage. The lion lacked charity. The young women chuckle and say goodbye.

Dallying. I must have missed by a minute or two seeing a cow give birth in a meadow by the sea.

a newborn calf
blood infused with sunlight
in its navel cord

In time though to see another episode in the cycle of life :

under different trees
two heifers and the bull
making up his mind

At a hundred-and-fifty yards, smiles of recognition beam down to
me, wind-sealed, from the party walking the ridge. I scramble up to complete
the rendezvous.

a good morning
shared without anyone
saying "Good morning" ...

gravelspin

all-day drizzle
yet bone-dry gravel
under Elgar's gate

          the torrent passes
          in soft slow ripples
          through the gills of fish

shorter days
     a crane-fly lays an egg
     in the mountainside

          the old spin bowler
          fingers twiddling
          in a bowl of sloes

midnight ... a moonbeam

Midnight ... a moonbeam
startles the magpie from its perch
a cool breeze stirs cicadas into chirp
and from blossoming paddy fields
inundations of fragrance
not to mention the muzzy croak of bull-frogs
have given the low-voiced farmers
a great deal to talk about ...

just seven or eight stars
are studding the firmament,
two or three raindrops, no more,
spatter the hillslope, before
whoosh! a summer downpour
drives me towards shelter ...

... an old familiar haunt!

I run towards the brook, I cross the bridge
and suddenly beside the wooden shrine
there is the tavern with its roof of thatch ...

... my eyes weep memories like grapes ooze wine!

after the Chinese of Hsin Ch'i-chi

the eaves hang low

The eaves hang low and lovely
with much-mended thatch
and shallow brooks are dappled
by the emerald grass. And then,
voices. Southerners.
From Wu, for sure,
easy enough to place
a burr like that!

Wish I could see them.

Aha, that couple, so advanced in years,
there in the arbour, getting drunk as lords!
Their drawl's enchanting,
while, on the stream's far bank, my eldest son
strides all about the beanfields,
hoeing weeds.
His brother plaits a good-sized chicken coop;
and my youngest,
so apt at finding nothing much to do,
lounges by the well, idly
splitting lotus pods.

after the Chinese of Hsin Ch'i-chi

29

larkfall

incoming tide
        the surfwatcher's shadow
                starts to float

                sciatica
           lying flat on my back
           I hear a lark

up above lark song
my daughter's
first-time parachute

           from eaves to earth
           raindrips trickle down
           the links of a chain

birthday dinner
lid of the ricepot
bubbling over

           I move like a saint –
           from pale green calyxes
           camellias fall

barbed parsnips *(parallel soliloquies)*

a tired flirtation
noticing slugs and snails
in lettuces

> ordinary day
> her spoon revolves slowly
> in the parsnip soup

evening by the river
red-painted toenails
slipping into silt

> a kiss on each cheek
> traffic tearing past
> in both directions

his mid-life crisis
purchasing valentines
three at a time

> barbed wire fences
> stretched across the moorland
> her tight lips

sleeping on my own
the quilt still wanders
his side of the bed

> breakfast in silence
> both halves of the grapefruit
> unsweetened

a visit to Boulge

The small church is buried in a clump of untidy trees. The first lane I take ends up in a breakers' yard run by travellers. The second lane is right, but blocked by a small lorry and an earth digger. Remaking pathways. Now almost lost in a quagmire threading between banks of wild snowdrops and aconites. The labourer with a shovel tells me at one funeral recently the bearers had to abandon the hearse and slither with the coffin half a mile to reach the church door.

The man knows nothing about the grave I've come to photograph. That it holds a famous poet does nothing to excite him. "Bloke who said we should have a good time while we can. You know, wine, women and song." A vague curl of the labourer's lip suggests that these are pleasures not unknown to him. "But hadn't much idea how to go about it," I add. "Mopy old bugger, actually." Almost a chuckle.

They have planted new roses and done something to put fresh vigour into the ancient one:

This tree raised in Kew Gardens from seed brought by William Simpson, Artist, Traveller, from the Grave of Omar Khayyam at Naishapur was planted by a few admirers of Edward FitzGerald in the name of the Omar Khayyam Club, 1893.

Some manure dolloped on it. There are still admirers.

> nature's call –
> my noonday pint flushes
> down an ivied yew

by nose to Hoxne

Names on the signposts don't tally with names on my map. This is North Suffolk, where folklore alerts us to expect such silliness. Well, I often get where I want to be by following my nose. Observe, just past midday, sun shining over my left shoulder, odds are I'm driving west-south-west. Should be fine to take me home, even though the B-road doesn't seem to be heading anywhere.

But we are still weeks short of the spring equinox. My angles wrong. The direction I've taken is in fact north-north-west, suddenly I'm three miles from a place I have always had an inkling to visit, but which usually seemed just that bit extra out of the way.

Hoxne. I wouldn't like to have to say it aloud, but I think it rhymes with 'oxen'. The tiny River Waveney bubbles through it.

Teetering through litter to take a photograph. There by the bridge is an inscription on a stone: *King Edmund taken prisoner here, A.D. 870.*

> emblazoned
> on a rusted pail
> early celandines

shadowhistle

into the dusk
that ends a century
    a roosting bird

               shadows along banks
               the medieval contours
               of our ancestors

   crows' wings
the shadows undulate
   over furrows

               autumn sowing –
               deep in a seed wheat sack
               the farmhand's whistle

St Edmund's Eve*

A north wind and heavy weather shorten the distance you could throw a spear. The sky black with the threat of snow; air laden with bonfire smoke, seeping through the ventilators into the car. Forest trees made solemn by a sudden overnight fall in temperature; dank leaves gleaming yellow. On the skyline, a wind turbine flailing against the approaching storm.

> out of the clouds
> in desperate flight
> the noonday moon

Behind a hearse and its accompanying limousine a line of slow-moving cars, a Jag, two Fords, an impatient Porsche. After three preparatory hops, a crow hoists up from the white line down the middle of the road.

> the merest shudder,
> more of the spines laid flat –
> a hedgehog skin

Such illumination as this day affords defines against a tree the pale outline of our first patron saint, Edmund, martyr, king of the East Angles. Strapped to a tree as a target and riddled with arrows by the heathen Dane, decapitated, head kicked into brambles half a mile from his body. They say it took forty days for monks to reassemble him.

That night, at my cottage, I see a film about English soldiers trying to keep peace in the Balkans. Theirs is not the 'camp' bravado of St George of the Caucasus, more the long-suffering tenacity of St Edmund of Bury, whom the dragon-slayer usurped. Soft but resistant. Like native clay and grit.

> this torso, this world
> the struggle to bring together
> head and heart

* St Edmund's Day is November 20th

35

snow bust

the stone image
accepts a light fall of snow
with lidded eyes

a lull in winter
the sexton pegs the sunshine
into portions

removing the moss
from *who passed away in peace*
I touch a nettle

unsure which is hers
I move the flowers about
from grave   to grave

turning from her grave
the tug of a rose thorn
on my padded sleeve

a bust of wet clay –
feeling one's own face
from the inside

hellbound (a round)

black sunrise
and the iridescent reek
of sulphur dew

on paper umbrellas
the hot precipitate
of human ash

we plunge into waterfalls –
the malodorous pain
of scalded shadows

ecstasy tablets
prescribed three times a day
till hell implodes

and spanish fly –
nude bellies straining
towards catheters

eat   eat   eat
in the isle of disease, and do not
neglect *les crudités*

with erect blue touch papers:
'Light the suppositories!' the red imp cries,
'And stand well back!'

bang! after each trip
the illusion
one's innocent again

the end of one day
beginning another   black sunrise ...

37

bagpiddler

Palm Court:
a down-at-heel quartet
take it out on Strauss

poky hotel
no room for my shadow
to unpack

the full moon glances
sideways down a street
of ill repute

Princes Street
rain piddling down
on the bagpiper

sceneshifters
for the opera's final act
talking football

stadium gents'
– the smell of cheering men
gone home

penalty
spot
clover

angel scars

in sunlight outside
the priest's hideaway
the power switch

             angels above
             the man in the sleeping bag –
                  cathedral front

fruit-crate
shelter in the scent
of orange groves

          this fly, so small
          inhabits a country
          with a huge world debt

his nails squeak also
      the Black teacher
      with the short chalk

             making a peg-leg
             for his pal, the leper
             grips with a scar

settling down

> shanty town
> in a yellow wheelbarrow
> someone very sick

"Okay, I'll settle for that."

What I've settled for this time is sixty. Actually, I'm seventy. Ten years ago, when I was really sixty, they guessed fifty. Twenty years ago, forty. They always underguess by ten years or more. The flattery is unintentional. Generally speaking, the world's children are not artful, they tell you mostly what they think they see.

This business of letting them ask me questions is part of checking what goes on in a foreign language classroom. It's pretty much routine.

"Where are you from?"

"How many children have you?"

"Are you married?" Sometimes, "How many wives have you got?" "Is your wife beautiful?"

Glancing at the teacher to see if it's polite, "How much do you earn?" The teacher smiles a blessing on the question because she too would like to know the answer.

And then, at some inevitable point, "How old are you?"

I've learned to deflect this blunt question with a question of my own, "How old do you *think* I am?" Trusting in the relic of a boyish face and a thirty-four inch waistline. And politeness to a visitor. They usually make an estimate I'm happy to accept.

The last question is, "Do you like Thailand?" Or Japan. Or Jordan. Or Nigeria. Or Namibia. Or Greece. Or Ghana. Or Singapore. Or Sierra Leone. I've had to answer it in all of those.

I tell the children wherever I happen to be that I love their country and them the best.

Which might really be true.

> she asks her question
> with a tongue of pure coral
> the girl with a worm

40

deliverance

In Jordan, monitoring the teaching of English in schools. "Prevention is butter than cure, by the Name of God", someone has written on the blackboard, next to a boy's sketch of a kalashnikov. The girls' headscarves are white as the teacher's chalk.

> by the prayer mat
> the sentry lays down his gun
> in line with Mecca

Wednesday. Three schools in Kerak, then to the Crusader castle, from whose walls Salah-ud-Din threw down the Christian commander, for his un-Christian behaviour towards Muslim girls. The cliffs too have been deflowered, step too near the unrailed windows and you may defenestrate yourself. Right onto the upbrandished scimitar of the Saracen's monument below. Urchins down there in the town square play football using a sarcophagus for a goal.

The night in the town's best small hotel. A truckle bed. Sweet lamb grill.

Thursday, to Tafileh. Twenty-five miles or so to the south, across a chasm.

> we pass from Moab
> into the Land of Edom
> without changing gear

Outflanking the town to get into it, we round a curving mountain terrace where El-Orens (of Arabia) ambushed and massacred a host of Turks and purloined their howitzers. Snow came down to blot the blood. Three schools this morning too. From the first of these my escort, the district English supervisor, a family man, despatches word home that I like fish. Not that I really do so much, but in answer to his question it's courteous. His wife is ready for us with a large fish at lunch-time. I catch a glimpse of her in the kitchen.

                an infant
                on her hip   the mother
                balances her scales

   She leaves her husband and me alone to deal with a feast for ten. Of
course, I think, she and the children will later eat up the remains; and then
she confounds my stereotypes by joining us for coffee. She talks well and is
expecting another baby.
   Friday. Twenty miles further south to Shaubak. End-of-week
atmosphere, a few hours to Friday prayers. We finish school visits early. My
escort of the day has a picnic for us, drives us up onto the hilltop citadel. I
unpack the carrier bags of gobbets of lamb, succulent bulbous onions,
unleavened bread, tomatoes of superb size and colour, water melons,
oranges, bottled water, hommous, while he gathers jetsam scraps of wood to
build a fire. As the meat grills, and I flirt with an Australian backpacker who
chances by, he strikes a pose on the ramparts and recites:

                Behold her, single in the field,
                Yon solitary Highland lass!
                Reaping and singing to herself;
                Stop here, or gently pass!

At two o'clock we are replete, the meal finishes with food to spare.

                a barren gorge
                under a kite's wings
                we bin our scraps

   My host wants to hurry home to Ma'an, I'm going to spend the
weekend in Petra. At the gates of some unidentified campus he drops me off,
tells me a bus will come.
   I am used to the workings of Providence in this holy land. The
buildings behind me identify themselves as a teacher training college, some
of the students, young men of eighteen, nineteen, twenty, nose me out, bring
me a wooden Windsor chair. I sit on it at the roadside and ask, "When will
the bus be coming?" The request is ignored in their interest about my age,
family, salary, and irregular verbs.

long wait for the bus –
on a goat's back some small bird
picks off a tick

Some time after four their tutor arrives in his car, shares with us the
joke about the bus to Petra. Not today or any other day. But he hasn't been
there himself, 50 miles away, for quite some time. Would be glad to take me.
Tells his wife so, and picks up a buddy to share the ride. My shoulder-bag of
books and papers, washbag and spare socks, are thrown onto the back seat.
So much desert, so much more interest in the photos in our wallets.
This your daughter? And fourteen? They bargain with me about her being a
bride for buddy on the back seat. Consent in principle is all they ask.

pecking the dust
of a village without fame
scrawny sparrows

The resthouse at Petra is cool in the April evening. The bar is a
manmade cavern, two thousand years old, a place where the Nabateans
stowed their dead and afterwards met up with them again for annual feasts. I
invite my saviours to join me for a drink, but no, they must head straight back
to Shaubak.

I shift my place-mat
to cover the dust of ages –
ice-cold beer

Middle of the night a scratch at the door, an unrecognized voice
sibillating through the keyhole, "Häh, sä-er, sä-er! please, it is I, sä-er! Open
for me, sä-er!" Head under pillow, I talk to my friends at Providence again,
knowing the door well locked.
At breakfast time the clerk at the front desk says, "Sir, your friend
from Shaubak came back in the night and left this for you." Something that
had fallen out of my washbag in the back of the car. He didn't discover it
until he had got back home.

43

The hotel clerk hands it to me. My toothbrush.

    the journey goes on
    I squeeze just that bit higher
    up the toothpaste tube ...

the wandering spring

The spring? ... well, obviously wandered off,
but where, where, leaving behind
the sort of loneliness that drains the will
even to look up friends.

Anyone with information
about this missing season
might do us all a favour ...

Perhaps only the golden oriole
could find the trail and spot the fugitive?
Downwind to the rose garden he flies,
this well-connected source,
sending back melodious bulletins,
but alas, who can make sense of
such babbled intelligence?

after the Chinese of Huang Ting-jian

whistlesmile

planning meeting
one jacket button
on a thread

                  lost in the country
           the roadmender points the way
                        with a mobile phone

                     above cow parsley
                     an eyebrow on a poster

                              – Mrs T's

                             polling day
                    swallows swooping
                    through a mist of flies

a pretty stranger
she more certain than me
how long to smile

             wine tasting –
             refilling my glass
             the flush of her blouse

               supper alone
               the chance to whistle
               through my macaroni

thistle tinder

every movement
      the grasshopper makes
            a leap in the light

trees move
only at their tips
midsummer dusk

rain butt bone-dry –
globe thistles like tinder
under the bees' feet

          after school homework
          about onomatopoeia
             the cough of a fox

sinslap

convent – on the line
a nun's wet black stockings
slap across my face

Cyprus, adieu –
        the backgammoners sit
        where they always sit

pre-flight check
a dead mosquito
on the ticket home

30,000 feet –
for a minute the Ganges
        bearing sins away

wind glimmer

late summer breeze
leaves of the book turning
before they are read

        sun setting
                the last glimmer
                Mr Punch's nose

the swifts have left
the silence
of the dusk

        first day at school
      in the garden only the wind
        swinging the swing

        no hunger for them
        but we pick the windfalls up
        out of respect

lapstone

After she snatched it
               right out of his lap, gave it away,
he adopted a stray round stone, with smooth-cut head,
a cob of flint, to be his new pet tabby.
It does not mew, shed hair, or come in season,
but sits close to his knee, and likes his care.
He feels his age, so does the lapstone,
A benefit to both this evening stroking.

At night he puts it out
into the cry of a little owl
wild over the ridge,
and in the morning it is there
waiting to be let in.

war memorials

Upon the village greens for ever
worthily staid the granite crosses,
but to remind of unimaginable
losses, I think of should-have-beens
such as a ragged shell-hole,
a sagging trench, and a rusting
cylinder of stench, certain
sure things to repel
and not about concealing
in the fall on a masked day
what we all need to recall:
the nasty feeling when you mix
shovelfuls of sticky mud with
about ten pints of blood.

sunfurrow

first morning of frost
steaming into the sunshine
a cat's yawn

                                                       black hips
narrow to the mouse-run –
autumn grass

                     across the fields of stubble
                              flame   stalks   flame

on a sloping field
motionless in furrows
wheels of straw

drip freeze

snow on the sill
the prisoner's finger
sneaking through the bars

confined too
the yellow wallflowers
by the prison fence

the lake frozen –
an extra twinkle
in a friend's glass eye

after the snowman
melts into the lawn
picking up his smile

drip
by
drip
moonlight
lengthens
in
the
icicle

scentmarks

in his clothes
for washing
       someone else's scent

car into gear
web-thread to the door
at breaking point

under the signature
the faint watermark
of a fish

at his funeral
his fellow councillors
sing in unison

letting the Bible
fall open as it will
       the Book of Job

during evensong
an inspiration to pray
Darken our lightness ...

empty chancel –
is there Someone who knows
I had to drop it?

second course

Next to me at dinner, seventeen and just half my age, the beautiful Eurasian girl, my ward for the voyage East. Daughter of an eminent Siamese surgeon, now dead of cancer, and a German mother returned since his passing to her fatherland and awkwardly remarried.

through a small circle   outside the porthole
of glass splashed with paint   the wing of a seagull
the open sea   keeping pace

Danish freighter. A few passengers. Seven weeks from Hamburg to Bangkok. On the first day, after a few hours' sailing, anchored. Rumoured the ship's engineer quarrelled with his governors in Copenhagen about our readiness to put to sea, and now, mid-German Ocean, is gloating. Under the full moon we rock on lugubrious waters.

decorous spooning
of cold Brown Windsor soup ...
the briny plankton

No shaft throb and propeller churn, but the rituals of meals go on. In the stillness, remarks at one table drift easily to its neighbour, and we, chosen today for the honour of sitting with the captain, are on our best behaviour. As we wait after removal of the soup dishes, my ward smiles, opens her pretty handbag, takes out a small silver box, beautifully chased. Like for snuff. She smiles a second time, ineffably, and opening the box over the empty space between my knife, fork and spoon, takes out a folded piece of paper. The next table struggle with their curiosity.

longer and longer
the cigarette in the holder's
plume of ash

"These are my father's," she explains, opening the paper and spreading before me, just where the waiter hesitates before placing a warmed dinner plate, some fragments of charred bone. The ash plume drops.

merit token

Northern Thailand. Visiting a temple on a mountain, Doi Suthep, where there are believed to be relics of the Buddha. Everyone, tourists as well as pilgrims, swinging logs at gongs to make them bong, releasing birds, sticking gold leaf all over the images, to feet, hands, noses and ears, right up to the Lord's topknot if they can reach that high, sometimes targeting that part of a buddha's anatomy where they themselves are afflicted.

Monsoon storm brewing. Wind snatching bits of goldleaf off the statues and whirling them in the air, a goldleaf autumn. Me, with my pinchpenny attitude, picking up one piece the size of a good round coin and placing it over the face of my watch. Now I can't read the time.

But rather soon it peels off. Twelve-thirty. I wonder where the little votive has gone to.

> on the latrine seat
> a small offering of gold
> from a buddha's thumb

> monsoon rain –
> visiting my girlfriend
> with the curse

55

clover ebb

drill squad
marching with fixed bayonets
into fog

even here a child
searching for four-leaf clovers
– on Culloden Moor

a torc of pine trees
all that now remains
of Boudicca's wrath

minutes of silence
into September ebbs
the Great Ouse river ...

army blankets –
traces of warriors'
wet dreams

Isandlwana

old battlefield
at dusk
a shivering light

wind into
dry dongas
piercing ice

hailstones lodge
in cairns scattered
where the fallen fell

blades of grass
parrying
the sleet

in snail shells also
the wind's brute entry
into secret coils

Isandlwana

a clatter of metal
in the litter bin
the ambush
of an empty can

of coke ...
no echo
from the Hat-like-Hill

the two of us silent
and without a shield
the Zulu and I stand
hand in hand

soldiers in flight

Mist shrouds the water,
moonlight sinks into mud.
Tonight our boat is moored
on the Chin Huai River
close to a tavern.
The girl they have paid to sing
knows nothing of our defeat,
that the nation is broken.
Her choice of song is all wrong:
"Flowers in the old backyard."

after the Chinese of Tu Mu

how they settled scores in the South China Sea

We, prisoners of war, in holds that are fetid,
hunkering, faring for feudal Japan.

They, lords of the sunrise, strutting the fo'castles,
drinking their rice-wine at dusk in a dream.

We in the heat's sway, a hundred and twenty,
we with no air but the breath of hot men.

They with the decks cool, orb slowly sinking,
sniffing, they swear it, the smells of Japan.

Hatches flung open: like spume of a man-whale,
we spew out our stenches, the evening invades

our offended unclothedness, frigidly kissed
by the gruel descending congealed in a pail.

Joyful, these colourless men, as each nightfall
ticks a day closer to Nippon their Mother;

only for us new alienation,
incarceration, different, same.

                    *   *   *   *

Wake of the shark that does not smell blood, now:
strike of torpedoes, the slave-ships on fire.

shudders that throw into boiling sea equal
jacketed, jacketless, captor and captive ...

Dead and alive flung afloat as companions,
all that ranks now is the power of their strokes.

Day of their dreams for those two from Down Under,
skin-and-bone mates with a scar in their grins,

apocalypse cobbers, who swim for their chances
to hunt their tormenters and teach them a dance,

homing on naval cap, targeting *kepi,*
they waltz the small sun-men and dunk down their heads

till bubbles no longer blip out of their noses,
till oil recoagulates where they went down.

A dozen they drown thus, in sweet vengeful murder,
revenge is so dear that they give it their hearts,

and will not desist till their lungs are unbellowed
and the last grain of strength from their sinews departs.

Then vortexing leadenly, sodden with gore-slick,
in the scum of their deadliness they too subside.

to the theatre

        to the end ward
        carpeting wall-to-wall
        a neutral colour

Will I be waiting in the day room, asks the Irish sister, explaining that she's top-heavy with males. I sit down next to a man who's embroidering Rupert Bears. "Took it up when I was last in here," he explains, "and now I'm onto my twelfth. It's catching." I take a firm grip of my newspaper.

At lunchtime a plate of hot food is placed under my nose, then whisked away. "Seeing as you're probably tomorrow," says the dinner lady. Charlie, who is 'family with the Queen' and pisses everybody off with it, is reluctant to leave, but finally gives up her side room to me.

        surgical bed
           trying to find the hollows
           where my bones fit in

Tagged, given pills 'to make me go', asked by my dedicated nurse if I am "All (as she opens the door) right? (as she shuts it again)". Hooked on the wall facing me a kind of leather strap with a label in bellicose capitals, PATIENT HANDLING SLING. Sleep at last.

A new day begins at six-thirty with the refilling of water jugs. I haven't been slung.

        morning of the 'op'
        changing the blade
        of my safety razor

Later, two jolly girls in green come to 'get me ready'. "Put on this, we're going to take you to the theatre." I tell them it will be my maiden trip.

        shivers down the spine
        making my debut
        in a backless gown

A stab in the back of my hand, a blood spot in the holiday tan, but not, they say, to make me sleep. Not yet. When you pass the *Restricted Entry* sign they start to squirt in the serious stuff.

> something injected –
> not hearing the end
> of my laughter

And then out of oblivion into consciousness again.

> cumulus clouds
> eyes add up the drips
> in the catheter

Being wheeled to a new berth, receiving flowers from the first visitors, vomiting, all at the same time. Flip sense of humour returning. Tell my little daughter, as some blood wriggles onto the floor and coagulates, this is how 'black puddings' are made. Six men eat their suppers in silence.

> "More gravy?" –
> the patients' conversation
> has dried up

When the lights go out, Mr Pobble (his toes have been amputated) commandeers attention. Pillows plumped up for him any time he wants, can even get his glass of water passed to him off the bedside table. When they bring him his commode we hear him complaining over the defences of drawn curtains, "I always face the wall. I want you to turn me round."

Morning again, and a visit from a nurse I don't recognise. "Just going to give you a quick flash," she says. Loosens the stopper of my catheter valve and tips something in. Tells me I shall feel a bit stiff. If only she knew how I am already, trying to enter the frigid constricted neck of the urine bottle.

The next nurse lifts the sheet, looks under it, says, "No, it isn't you I'm looking for", goes away, comes back, and then says, "Sorry, it *is* you, but it's your bum I want, not *that*. Please turn over."

                    burdensome heat
                    a fly slowly circles
                    my sticking plaster

    Rounds. The registrar discusses with the Irish sister whether I am
nauseating. They decide to give me the benefit of the doubt. On the third day
I rise again and get a taxi to my own bed. From it, the old familiar landscape,
but through new spider webs.

                    midnight chimes –
                    I count even those strokes
                    the traffic drowns

whinnycress

for their retirement
first purchase with the pension
'reproduction beds' ...

in the bedroom mirror
the old slow bowler
bowling at himself

from the ridge, whinnies
of an old long-coated horse
long while coming down

grannie's album
centre of each snap
her fingerprint

her careworn hands
wrinkling exactitude
into watercress

remorseless frost
the first uneaten berries
closer to the house

dementia
a thin light disperses
through venetian blinds

women, dying

The wish to die and the will to live. Her eyes beseeching me to wet her lips, her lips when wet beseeching me to 'slip her something to be out of it all quick.'

Such women of our breed, with their long, fighting deaths, gritting their toothless gums as each new morning forces itself in through the chinks of drawn blinds, whiskery-chinned. Some instinct to maintain things and die holding a cup of tea. To do what is needful and do it without fuss.

A man might learn something from them he can't learn from another man.

>   as she lies dying
>   I tell her the crocuses
>   are early this year
>
>   at the Gates of Eternity
>   I take her hand and say,
>   'It snows in Essex ...'

testaments

bend in the river
        the longboat
                straightens for the lock

                a misshapen apple:
                        I end up cutting it
            into five
                  quarters ...

far as eye can see
the beach   holding tight
                to three feet of rope

A DAY IN TWILIGHT

a day in twilight

Mythical beings share intuitions with us and desire our company?

Taken with this idea and feeling sure their need would be greatest when days are short, I determined, as it was the winter solstice, to seek some of those beings out; persuading myself there was no better time to do so, nor any more poetic time, than this. In the continuous twilight it might happen that I should find myself in company with men and women who had perhaps never been, or never were as they are now told to have been, but yet seem palpable in mossy Essex.

> in the creases
> of an Ordnance map, flicker
> of an open fire

Old King Coel it was whom I had most in mind, that merry old soul last embodied a hundred years ago whilst partaking of the Oyster Feast at Colchester, in the divine company of Emperor Claudius, as well as the royal company of Kings Cymbeline, Cassivelaunus and Caractacus, Queen Boudicca and Aulus Plautius the Roman Governor of Britain, Godric the Saxon and Athelstan, together with a bevy of low churchmen and high cavaliers. All linking hands together, singing *For he's a jolly good fellow.* [1]

> a merry company –
> they sit at a round table
> in square chairs

But though Colchester is so old a city [2] that Noah is said to have sailed into its port in the Ark, which may be proved by the success of the zoo there in mating a zebra with a donkey and producing a pair of zedonks, I preferred to seach for Coel in rustic surroundings. In a town one may easily suffocate in the search for certain people living in certain buildings at certain times, when all people of any real consequence [3] inhabit the air around us, indifferently, and we might hope to respond to this inhabited air as sensitively as an Aeolian harp to the slightest wind.

in the hug of darkness
the intimacy
of tree with tree

I dress before dawn, no very unlikely thing to do on December's twenty-second day, night making way slowly for the gloom which at this time of year we are pleased to call daylight. "Fog," says the radio, reducing visibility to a hundred metres. About a furlong away on the ridge are outlines which, though nebulous, I know to be sturdy trees. The man on the radio taking only the minus view, of things that are removed from our sight by fog, not of things that are given.

bedraggled dawn	morning at last –
the grey nextdoor cat	switching on a light
mews to be let in	to see it better

Impetuosity argues with discretion, caution with scorn of consequence, until my foot puts itself down to settle the matter; and so I set out, *avec mon sang froid habituel,* otherwise the usual bloody cold that begins the Yuletide season . [4]

Porridge swells my belly, a rucksack rubs my collarbones. For a few strides the illusion my head is ten feet above the ground, but a hundred yards or so and I've shrunk to my own true size again; being in two miles just another huddled small beast of the countryside. Skirt the ford some say named for Saelred, one-time king of these parts, [5] and turn at the first chance off the main road into Hull's Lane, named for a smallholder who kept pigs in a copse nearby. I walk in the middle of the lane. Soon it becomes a holloway, but at first its one edge cambers away down a cliff into a boggy dip, the other edge is overhung with straggling hollies and shameful elders. [6]

Stench. A poultry-farmer has created a new highpoint on the horizon with a hillock of turkey-muck. From tractor wheels, droppings welt-deep. In a county where twenty-two inches is reckoned a wet year, the council leaves the cleansing of a sunken lane to rain. A mobile phone mast mimics a balding cedar tree. Cackle from a disturbed scavenging bird.

magpie, so furtive –
you know no one
thinks you did it

Windtangle of old man's beard over neglected hedges. Foul ditches. On verges of the lane newly-sprung grasses pierce through herbage rotted by the frosts. Now a line of oak trees compose themselves in a variety of eccentric but for them comfortable postures. Like venerable seniors slumped before a cold grate, I feel they demand a lullaby:

Rest, hoary oaks!
Your acorns are sown.
Far from the ink-gall
The worm, it is flown.
Your boughs, they are wind-gnawn,
The magpie's alone.
Sleep, hoary oak,
Till the winter is done!

Past ditches delved out by medieval hands and further scalloped by rough weather, I avoid at Waltham's Cross the turning to Wethersfield, though for the moment there is the temptation that in that village there may still be a woman descended from the Barbara who, some two and a half centuries ago, according to her monument, "faithfully practised all the duties proper to her sex and station through the several stages of a long life." [7]

A steep contour. Soles of boots squeak as they descend the slope into the cottage-rimmed green dell of Finchingfield. By the narrow humped brick bridge at the neck of the duck pond I halt to let a rider pass by on a white horse. She reins it in on the crown of the arch and bending down from her saddle asks me the way to Steeple Bumpstead. "Kind sir," she adds.

Me, a kind sir, in my tramping clothes. I sketch a bow.

Behind me, to the right, I tell her, confused; no, to the left, for we are looking each other in the face. "Up past the old white weatherboarded windmill."

"Old?" she queries, when she is at the corner and the post mill comes in view. [8]

"For you it may have a very new look," I concede.

The lady on the white horse will be a pilgrim, I surmise. [9] On her way to Bury, where she may invoke Saint Edmund to help her bear a child; or the better to endure her hammer toes. Edmund – paragon of those most English virtues, endurance and losing with grace. Prince of sufferers, our original patron saint. She will believe whatever the monks tell her about him.

> martyr's shrine:
> the verger dusts it
> just enough

The verse changes in my head from a casual reminiscence to a metaphor of memory itself.

It was Normans who supplanted Saint Edmund with Saint George. Yet he clings on, not quite redundant but almost undercover; preserving us, for example, from the awful realisation that tidy little vegetable gardens of some council houses are growing on mass graves of the Black Dead. Deadman's Lane mumbled into St Edmund's Lane. [10] As for Edmund's own bits and pieces, broken up by Ivar the Boneless, no one really knows where they are. [11]

> small winter sun –
> the sexton
> with a ball of string

"That lady on a horse, she'll be on her way to Bury," I inform the woman in the café where I call in for a hot tea and scone.

"We're just back from the Canaries, ourselves," she responds. I observe her bare arms that tone in with the just-cut coffee-cake from which she is lifting the first carefully considered slice. "In the summer we were in Turkey and in Florida in the spring."

Essex, England, places to escape from, and so often? She brushes crumbs from the table, brings the bill, I leave, passing a house called *Saxons*.

"Never been nowhere else, mysel'," grumbles a good-natured, guttural voice over my shoulder. It must be Old Fink, said to have given his name to this village, no doubt convinced there is no better place to be. [12]

"Can you tell me the name of this stream?" I ask.

71

"We jus' call un Stream. Tis no more'n a babblin' owd brook with a titchy little pond or tew. But in a mile – you know what a mile be? – ut mixes itsel' with the right owd river what we call Pant. My grandfather learned me the name. Said we was to call un so because names mus' never go to waste, even names bestowed by those Welsh folk what jabber away wholly in their own sing-song as all us know."

"Pant is their word for 'boggy valley'," [13] I reprove him, lapsing into my habitual pedantry. "But we agree on essentials. Pant is still the name of our river here and it should be fought for to keep it so. Now then, while we're talking of the mystery of names, will you tell me how it came about that Finchingfield was named for you?"

"First tell me your own name. Then I may tell."

I give him my name.

"What, Cobba, you don' say?" Guffaws beat a tattoo on his diaphragm. "Runt like yew cheeky enough to go about callin' hisself a great leadin' man? Why, they was havin' yew on!" I tell him I've heard nicknames are often to be understood arsy-versy. [14]

"As for me," he goes on, "yew may think my father, seein' me nippy at my mother's breasts, snufflin' about like, was took with a thought of a small bird o' the hedgerow, twitterin' and spadgerin' from twig to twig, while wind was a-blowerin', and so he called me Fink, which as you may know is 'finch'? No. 'Twas because the village folk thought me uncommon frisky after women. Like a cock dunnock; lewd, you see! I supped my nettle broth and had horn by the bloody ell. More 'n a wren's tail, 't any rate!" [15]

> a mongrel digs
> in a bare flower border
> for a summer bone

"Long time sin' I had the horn," says Fink, in a misty parenthesis. "Lot longer than yis'ty mornin'."

Brightening, he goes on: "But the times an' times Freya [16] were good to me! Give me a wife what bore well. And hogs scrabbled in the beech mast deep as yer elbow and their little owd piglets done work hard at the sows' dugs and my own chillun sucked good, tew. Yes, it were me makin' out half-tidy what got folk around to settlin' my name upon this place."

"There was Winfred as we called Cat's-Beard and Athelhort what was known as Boghound. Likely they might of named this town for any o' we three, but them tew wasn't spared for no long life. One struck by Thor's bolt under a blasted elm tree while out gettin' moss to wipe his arse on, t'other laid open by his own little owd iron axe while choppin' up an elder tree, and the wound turnin' wicked with black stinkin' pus. Me now, never took no harm at all, had a sight o' luck."

"And did you get on well with your wife?" I interject. "You say you were lusty in your prime and had a roving eye."

"Oh, ah, she were a reg'lar good owd gal. Done as I tell her to. Let *me* do as I'd a fancy to."

"Marriage has a strange history around about here," I muse aloud. "But what would you know, Old Fink, about a man who tilled your yardland a thousand years after your ploughshares had gone to rust? [17] Published his wife as an adulteress and then found out he had done so in error, swore to punish himself by holding his tongue for seven years. Two years into his penance his wife died, but dumb he remained five years more, keeping his vow to her until it had run its time. Then fell mortally ill. From his sickbed, tried to call out for help, but died on the spot; died of shock; after all those years of keeping silent he had lost his voice!"

"Nettles, again," comments Fink enigmatically. "Had he made his wife drink nettle pottage mixed with ale, he'd never 've fallen for this lie and gotten hisself stucken in that sort o' dungpot. S'pose she weren't doin' no wrong? Then she'd 've kept the drink down, every whole last drop what she swallowed, and then he'd 've got to the trew bottom o' things." I sense there is no arguing with an honest old East Saxon about the efficacy of nettles.

Fink asks me where I am going and I tell him to see Old King Coel.

"Bartlow Hills, mebbe?" he says with a quietness that hints at misgiving. "Reg'lar scary owd place, that, they do say. Mebbe see you there, though, later on." Shakes his head and, like the Cheshire cat, he disappears.

Out of the dip of pale ancient winter morning light, where cottages hem things in, up to the broader outlook of fields.

> plodding, prodding –
> together as we walk
> the stick and I

Trudging up to Brent Hall. A partridge pecks the driveway, its red legs scatter a pebble or two of gravel.

"Allow me, sir, if you will." A woebegone figure, wearing breeches with faded embroidery and a slash-sleeved jacket that was once lined with bright colour, has insinuated himself from nowhere and now by my side is giving a demonstration of 'palely loitering'. There are faded roses on his shoes and he has a pockmarked face.

"I saw you, sir, a moment ago, writing in your pocketbook and, being a poet myself, take you for one of our harmless fraternity. Let me introduce myself, sir: Benlowes, Edward Benlowes. Benvolus, I ask my friends to call me. Born in this hall and lived here nearly all my life." We nod ourselves into acquaintance. He is right enough. I had observed something out of the nook of my eye, taken out pencil and paper and scribbled down:

> over the furrows
> undulating shadows –
> slow flaps of a crow

Self-piteously, Benvolus continues, "My fate has been one of the hardest poet ever bore. I shall die without food or fire, my estates sold to print my books or to pay fines – I took the losing side in the King's war with Parliament, you know. All I have to show for my life is short editions, and the respect of a very few of my peers."

"Many of our fraternity fare no better."

"Have you ever read my book?" [18]

"Yes, I borrowed it from the library once." Something close to my heart urges me not to tell him that, ninety years and more after that copy had been printed, I had to cut its pages. Nor that, when I went to return it, the library had locked its doors early, as if they were not so keen to have it back.

"Benvolus," I say, laying my hand on his insubstantial shoulder, "few English poets have had better fortune than you, most were not even noticed. We are a nation that pride ourselves on our literature, and are prepared to pay sixpence for it if we can't get it for fourpence."

Shaking his head, then brightening, Benvolus enquires, "Will you now kindly show me your poem, sir? I should like to see if I have any influence on you poets who come after me."

I show him the draft of my haiku. "Why, sir," he claps his hands, "I conceive that like me you prefer syllabic verse. In three-line stanzas, too, by glorious Jove!"

I recall that Benlowes wrote in triplets of ten syllables, followed by eight syllables, then twelve.

"But I fear you have strayed far from my measure, sir. A sufficient number of syllables is lacking, you race to your point, sir, like a hound that has the smell of a bitch on heat. And your rhymes – *shadows* and *furrows* will not do with *crow*. Now, let me see, had I the turning of your lines – you will indulge me? – they would be more on this wise." He cocks one velvet leg against a tree stump and in this pose starts to recite:

> Sol, in Earth's dim wardrobe, garments flings
> Of sable stripp'd from a Rook's wings,
> Striping undulant ground that snail-like Ploughman prings.

I ponder whether I should give my earnest companion a lecture on the poetics of a land he probably knows as Chipangu,[19] decide instead to exercise restraint. He has, after all, fastened onto my word *undulate,* which has a fine poetic ring, he declares. Something our ears share across three or four hundred years.

"I think you will be turning left here," I say, "whilst I shall be going straight on."

> two bold cock robins –
> everything within strict bounds
> except their songs

Even on a day of modest wind there is chill air across the small-scale ridgeland prairie where I now find myself. Set against a line of dark slender limes, like a lace jabot on a black collar, the eastern end of Little Sampford church. Mouldering. Its floor made of damp loose yellow bricks.

> honey for sale –
> all my loose change tipped out
> on a quiet hive

75

Someone's Christmas present, maybe, I tuck it into my knapsack. A moment or two later I come to Sparepenny Lane. Great Sampford. Its pub gutted by fire some years ago, then restored. Should be a *Phoenix*, but keeping the old sign, *Red Lion*, a lion with wings, triangular like spoilers, more to improve the beast's roadholding, you would think, than help it fly. And why would it wish to fly, in this sky marred with the gross graffiti of all those electric power lines?

> a file of pylons
> the power in the land
> of Gog and Magog [20]

"Village needs more buses," I overhear someone queuing in the shelter. "To keep they rabbits down." There is an animal cadaver with a cottonwool tail squashed in the middle of the road, waiting for a scavenger. I take refuge on the green path, in places elevated above the metalled way to the height of a man's shoulders. When the path runs out, a postwoman's head pops out of a gap between ten-foot hedges, nervously checking if it is safe to cross the road to reach her bicycle. Cars are passing, as they say locally, 'of a tidy speed.' With tense eyebrows the postwoman and I exchange 'good mornings'. Then a driver pulls up and offers me a lift. Surprised into aimlessness, I accept, before realising that his route will take me off on a detour. Inside the car it is hot as pipe smoke and there is banshee music from the local radio. I ask to be dropped off at Radwinter.

> anonymous road:
> December's ash-tree keys
> shall be your name

Radwinter, where a Saxon woman possibly named Raedwynn had something to do with some kind of tree. [21]

"Oh, Raedwynn, why do I glimpse you, there by the river under a willow, with your long undressed hair trailing into the water?"

"Maybe I drowned, do you think? No, you do not see me about to take my life or lose it, nor do you even see me at all. It is my unwed mother you see, weeping. She has lain me in a basket of woven osiers and set me adrift on the flow. Now it is tears of remorse that trickle down her cheeks.

But there is no need. A swan is already swimming the basket back to her, soon she will have me again at her breast, and then she will cherish me."

Lying on the ground near a litter-bin, some take-away food wrapped in newspaper.

'... a nation's grief ...' –
leaking through the headlines
greasy chips

The rectory at Radwinter for sale. *Inspection Invited.* My curiosity tickled by this to see the famous Elizabethan pastor's dwelling, even if the time so spent means I must walk faster for the rest of the day. [22]

cold dew –
my fingertips condense
on the knocker

My summons brings Master William Harrison himself to the door. There is an odour of stale coffee that neither of us likes nor can account for. He apologises for the huge brick fireplace too.

"A mistake, sir, having that put in," he pleads. Dismisses it with a gesture and, sniffing the air, hints how much more pleasant it had been when the smoke from smouldering logs had eddied around the hall.

He invites me to ascend the almost vertical ladder to his chamber. Not without confusion, for when I say 'ladder' he understands me to refer to 'shelves', and when I say 'stairs' he takes it amiss that I should apparently have in mind to climb the stool-sized set of steps that take me right into his bed. At last, from a rung or two below me, the stern warning, "Let not your foot stutter, sir, for I am just behind you, my Bible in one hand and a lighted candle in the other!" I cling to the side-ropes with a desperate faith.

"Did you never feel, Master Harrison, as you climbed aloft at night, that you were on your way to heaven?"

"Fie, sir, mistake a flock mattress for Paradise? Nay, for I have ever considered such dainties to be impediments to health in this our mortal domain, and to our future grace."

"I have read in your book that you also have strong things to say about fashions in clothes. 'Fantastical folly' is, I think, your phrase."

"Words I own to, sir."

"You find the garb I'm wearing rather odd?" I imagine some phrase like 'dolorous disarray' is passing through his mind.

"I do not make you out, sir. Your speech might be that of a man who has been to the seashores of Bohemia, [23] but your apparel does not fetch from there. It has both the stoutness of work, and the softness of play. I trust you are honest, not some levelling preacher. A husbandman's son, maybe, that inherited no wealth, and went to the New World to seek his fortune, adopting the fashions of an Indies man?"

I try to explain that jeans and anorak are new fashions for the road, indulged in the lower parts of Essex, and don't tell that I am in fact descended from a husbandman, thirty years his senior, [24] who was but recently (three hundred and fifty years ago) summoned before the Court of Star Chamber to answer for joining in a riot against the enclosure of some common land. He might preach at me, taking as his text *Exodus chapter 22, verse 5.* [25] Nor do I tell him about the landowner I heard just last week on the TV, arguing against more freedom to roam the countryside, "We don't want it all turned into a dog's lavatory, now do we?" Meanwhile, his own cows squittering over a public right of way.

dreams
in a dormant field –
an inch of wheat

"I wish you a commodious and most easy passage," Master Harrison bids me farewell, glad I think to be rid of someone who might be a vagrant and in earnest need of a whipping, or even the mischievous spawn of John Ball. I edge my way out of his garden that merges without perceptible boundary into the adjacent churchyard.

molehills:
the sexton looks at them
(he says) two ways ...

Out of Radwinter to Gallows Farm and a turning towards Hempstead. The highwayman Dick Turpin born here at *The Bluebell Inn.* [26] Half a mile down the byway, I catch hold of a crooked blackthorn stick only to find on the other end of it someone who also had a mind to pick it up.

"Hey, that there's mine!" says the young ruffian who is practising the art of hold-ups this short, murky afternoon. I see the crooked stick looks like a pistol and am not surprised. "I 'opes, sir, as yew ain't no odstropolous owd sod? Stan' an' deliver! That's what I gotta say. Stan' an' deliver! Show us your possesshuns."

I slip the knapsack from my shoulders and loosen the drawstrings. The stripling rummages through the contents.

"Pair o' ankle-jacks, [27] rare lot o' linen. Fancy drawers like a lady o' the court might stuff 'er bum in. Faith, you're a rum 'un! Not a lot 'ere what a gen'leman o' the road, as I aim to be, might wear. Potta honey, too. And what's this? Hard jam?" He wipes the stickiness of pressed, pitted dates onto his hand-me-down tricorne hat.

Delving deeper, his hand makes contact with a softdrink can.

"What we got 'ere? Canteen o' something? Rum toddy or the likes?"

"It's coke," I assure him. He raises an eyebrow.

"Ow'd yew get it open, then?" He tucks the blackthorn pistol between his knees and tries to unscrew the top of the can, until I gesture to him to lift the ring pull. He gives a sharp tug. Froth erupts from the broken seal and the would-be highwayman evaporates in a spray of cola. I pick up the pistol and throw it to a passing dog. The dog fawns on me and follows me to *The Bluebell.*

<blockquote>
on the inn hearth
a poker for the ashes
... old men's gossip
</blockquote>

In Turpin's inglenook sits a retired gent who has just boasted to his companion that he once played walk-on parts in several TV soap operas and claims he is an eccentric. He wears a brown hacking jacket, grey flannels, a grey woollen cardigan, English brogues, all a sensible match, and has discarded a tartan scarf and the sort of felt hat in which anglers pin their flies. His crony's attire is rather similar. "Yes," he concludes, "eccentric is the right word for me. Bohemian."

The other man has meanwhile turned his attention to his crisp bag. "Fifteen percent more now," he informs his bosom friend.

"Yes, but fifteen percent more of *what?* Likely as not it's just fifteen percent more bag!" The eccentrics add their litter to the pile in the chimney-piece.

As I leave, I let the fawning dog pick me up again and meander back with him to the main road. To entertain him, I tell him about the 'young dog' who said, "Poets live and walk with their poems; a man with visions needs no other company." [28]

"He was wrong, of course," I add hastily, but the mongrel has already taken umbrage and made off, sniffing, through a gap in the nearest hedge. I carry on alone to a crossroads where there are roadworks and a set of traffic lights. The lights are at red, but they have no cars to stop.

held up
low in the road ahead
an amber sun

Damp. At most signposts pausing to wipe my glasses. Chilly. Behind every tenth hedge stopping for a leak. I wonder about sending all the loves of my life postcards from a ploughed field, "Do not wish you were here." Then I pull my zip like a funicular to its top.

a final twirl
and the last thin leaf
slides into free fall

Through discarded sycamore leaves covering a flat bridge over the stony bed of a dry bourne I rustle, almost treading on the tail of a cock pheasant which wheezes and clatters aloft in its surprise, giving the impression of bagpipes slung through the air, just managing to skirl over a four-foot-six high wall. Hampered by notices of *Private Ground.* Embers of setting sun reflect in cumulus clouds.

I mount a wooden stair of sixty-three steps to the summit of the largest of the Bartlow Hills. [29] From the top I look down on three smaller mounds, one cut through as it had been cheese by some uncompromising railway engineer aiming for the quickest route to Cambridge. The abandoned cutting, with its detritus of fallen leaves, affects me with melancholy, and I also need to pass water once again. It is raining a bit, and when the gods give no better example of bladder control, what can a mortal do? I decide to make my aim the sky. [30]

                    from the prepuce
                    disclosing a coy glans –
                    the man in the moon

An old dulled sickle. A scalpel of steely light. I shiver and my urine falls waywardly. "Not much of a shot, am I?" I apologize, adding with more courtly propriety, "Pardon, Your Majesty. An anti-climax." For I am aware, after all, it is under this, the major Bartlow Hill, that Old King Coel is supposed to be taking his eternal rest. "I think Your Majesty can take a jest," I plead. "They say you were a merry old soul."

Something like a mournful sigh proceeds, I think, from mid-mound. "If only a man could write his own nursery rhymes about himself!" says the sigh. "Let me tell you now, I did enjoy many a bowl of Gallic wine – and got the gout from it! Pipe? Nobody in my day smoked anything, not even bramble leaves. As for the pleasure of listening to fiddlers – do you know when the violin was invented? My men played the *harp* to me. And not very good at keeping in tune. But fortunately I was almost stone-deaf by the age of thirty-two, though deafness isn't normally an occupational hazard of kings. Well, I enjoyed watching their fingers on the strings. We used to say, a man needs only three things for his contentment – a harp, a chaste wife, and a cushion for his seat. I had all three." [31]

"It was a golden age?" I venture. I imagine his musicians playing Offenbach.

"Golden? It was an age of almost such drab mediocrity as your own. Less cant and less tinsel, maybe. I worked to one simple rule: if you let popular appeal determine what's entertaining, it soon comes down to pouring muck over people's heads."

Again the wrangle in my heart between the common and the noble touch.

"We have just made something like your mound," I tell the king, "but much, much bigger. It's to inspire our future and uses as its symbol fingers crossed." I spare Old Coel any more detail. He also was around once at the start of a new millennium.

The mound is silent. "Visits like mine ... get on your nerves?" I hesitate.

Something between a hiccup and a chuckle. "Do you know what my jester used to say? The living haunt the dead far more than the dead haunt the living."

> stretched on barbed wire
> the grin in a hare's skull –
> oh, Eulenspiegel!

The wind seems to blow the moon in and out of clouds and I recall some words I doubt Old Coel knows, words of a man with a very big nose. [32]

"Your Majesty, I wonder if you can see that moon up there? I think it possible. Once I read a book, by a man who pretended to have been to that very moon, in which he said a man has in him everything he needs to resurrect himself as a tree. Such a man can surely see the sky through a hillock of soil?" And I go on, "Something else that writer put in his book: 'All is in all; that is to say, in water there is fire, in fire there is water, in air there is earth, and in earth there is air.'"

The monarch ponders a moment. "As the wit said, everything is in everything, and vice versa. You could say, a man passes through worms and becomes soil of the moon, for moon-soil is no different from myth."

> folds of a ditch –
> the sort an unshaven man
> could fall in love with

"You didn't mind becoming a myth?" I ask the king.

"Better than going down in history," he replies sedately. "History is depressing, but myths uplift us. We may look forward to our resurrection as imaginary beings, but not to reincarnation. " [33]

> nearby in the dark
> someone calls someone else
> using my name

I descend the sixty-three steps and traverse the unkempt churchyard to Bartlow church. It has a wall painting of Saint George and the Dragon, only some offending hand has coated the saint in thin whitewash, and deprived of its adversary, the Dragon's fiery breath has turned to pallid steam.

I climb into the pulpit, intent on preaching myself a sermon, but only this commandment occurs, "Thou shalt follow thy nose."

In the gathering dusk a painted board with its last word broken off: 'Beware of the ...'. So to an inn, *The Three Hills,* and the smell of hops.

> a wooden bench
> chewed by worm and wasp –
> my weary legs

As I slowly sip my beer I resolve that, having more or less walked the Old Year out, I shall not trouble to walk the New Year in. Yet a journey like the one I have just made may be one of an infinite number that the Guiding-Following Spirit dreams, in *our* heads, it is making every moment of time. That is, if we can make the imaginative leap to the belief that we are vessels of the Everwakeful-Sleep. Taking part not only in the process of physical evolution which we all learn about at school, but also in a process of spiritual evolution whose essential mechanism is Survival of the Fittest Dreams.

"Buggered for a tale!" grunts Old Fink scornfully. He has crept in from the woods, smelling of pig dung and beech mast, and has already followed *his* nose into a pint of Old Bob. His tongue, loosening in the froth, offers his opinion that the gods use us for their sport. For a moment I might have mistaken him for Prometheus.

But didn't Shelley speculate that poets of all ages contributed to one Great Poem perpetually in progress? [34]

How can I share with Fink my earnest hope that, when scientists have artificial intelligence almost in the bag, they will never be able to lay their hands on artificial intuition? Some hope then for poets.

While Fink and I finish off our beers, I phone home and ask to be fetched. We give the old Saxon a lift back to Finchingfield, on condition that I give the inside of the car a good scrub next day. Reaching home, I change into fresh clean clothes like those worn by the gentlemen in Hempstead pub.

> the shortest day –
> almost no time at all
> to have a shadow

notes to 'A day in twilight'

[1] *Old King Coel ... in the divine company ...:* a fair description of the assembly depicted on the toast-list for the Colchester Oyster feast of 1899.

[2] *Colchester ... so old a city:* Geoffrey of Monmouth, C12th historian, is the prime source for the belief that England's oldest city is named after Coel. The British name was Camulodunon. *Oxford Dictionary of Place Names* says Colchester means 'the Roman station on the River Colne', but adds that the etymology of 'Colne' is obscure, though of British origin and originally 'Colun'.

[3] *all people of any real consequence:* the germ of this idea is in Marx's *Das Kapital* – 'All that is solid melts into air.'

[4] *sang froid = bloody cold:* a classic schoolboy howler.

[5] *Saelred:* King of Essex, 709-746 AD. Some say 'Shalford' derives from 'Saelred's ford', though 'shallow ford' is much more obvious.

[6] *shameful elders:* elder was considered the Tree of Disgrace, as it provided the wood from which Christ's cross was made. Thought also to be home of the Elder Witch, who should be treated with respect. When felling an elder it was prudent for the woodsman to say, "Owd girl, give me of thy wood, and I will give thee some of mine when I grow into a tree."

[7] *the Barbara:* Barbara Mott, d. about 1715, memorial in Wethersfield church.

[8] *the post mill:* the present mill dates from the C18th, later than the time of pilgrimages, but it was the successor to earlier mills.

[9] *The lady on her white horse ... on her way to Bury:* Finchingfield and Steeple Bumpstead lay on a pilgrim's route to Bury St Edmund's.

[10] *Deadman's Lane = St Edmund's Lane:* there is an example of this corruption on the outskirts of Great Dunmow, Essex.

[11] *Ivar the Boneless:* commander of the mid-ninth century Danish force that rampaged through East Anglia and put Edmund, King of East Anglia, to death, because he would not renounce his Christianity.

[12] *Old Fink, who is said to have given his name to this village:* according to *Oxford Book of Place Names,* the name means 'the *feld* of Finc or his people. Finc is recorded as a pre-Conquest Saxon by-name, sometimes given to a simpleton.' Coincidentally, the house nearest to Finchingfield stream and duckpond bears the name *Saxons* to this day.

[13] *Pant is their word for 'boggy valley':* Or 'boggy hollow'. Boggy places were regarded by Iron Age Celts as portals of a watery underworld where powerful divinities lived, to be propitiated by human sacrifices that had suffered a 'threefold death' (a blow, a stab, and strangulation).

[14] *What, Cobba, you don' say?:* P H Reaney, *Dictionary of British Surnames,* explains the author's surname thus: 'Cobb, Cobbe, from Old English *cobba* = 'big, leading man', an original nickname.'

[15] *I supped my nettle broth:* Fink's folk wisdom about the aphrodisiac properties of the common stinging nettle was not put down on paper until Andrew Borde did so in the reign of Henry VIII: 'yf any married man the whych would have this matter or desyre and can not thorowe imbecyllyte use the act of matrimony ... in the mornynge use to eat II or III new layd eggs rosted, and put into them the pouder of the sedes of nettles with sugar. But nowe a dayes few hath this impediment, but hath erection of the yerde to synne. A remedy for that is to leape into a great vessell of colde water or to put nettles in the cod pece about the yerde and stones.' Naturally, Fink was brought up to prefer a Saxon expression like 'horn' to one of Latin origin, like

'erection'. Another concoction containing nettle extract was recommended by the herbalists to detect whether a girl's maidenhead was intact. Fink's suggestion that it might also be used as a test of chastity is not documented, but seems in line with other beliefs. See Pamela Mitchell, *All Good Things Around Us*, 1980.

[16] *Freya:* Saxon goddess of love.

[17] *a man who ploughed your yardland:* William Kempe, C16th owner of Spains Hall, Finchingfield, a patron of zealous Puritans.

[18] *Have you ever read my book?:* Edward Benlowes, b. Brent Hall, Finchingfield, 12 July 1602, is known (if at all) for his 'divine poem' in 12 cantos, *Theophila, or Love's Sacrifice*, published (or rather, self-published) in 1652. It describes the progress of a soul towards Heaven. For a full life, see Harold Jenkins, *Edward Benlowes*, Athlone Press, 1952. Says the *Oxford Companion to English Literature*, 'the poem, written in successive triplets of ten, eight, and twelve syllables, uses curious coinages of words and phrases' and was 'ridiculed by Samuel Butler, Pope, and Warburton.' G. Saintsbury, in *Minor Poets of the Caroline Period*, 1905, describes Benlowes' favourite form as giving a 'jolt which only after long familiarity becomes rhythmical even to the most patient and experienced ear, and never reaches a perfect charm.' North-west Essex has something of a tradition of dubious poetical innovations: Gabriel Harvey, of Saffron Walden, in the time of Elizabeth I, pronounced the future of English poetry to rest with the hexameter; and of the present author, Cobb, the less said the better. It might be said that the section titles in *Palm* ('nettlebuzz', 'codpoppies', etc.) are not unlike the curious compounds that Benlowes loved to invent (such as 'dwarf-words', 'wormships') though any similarity occurred spontaneously.

[19] *a land he probably knows as Chipangu:* maps contemporary with Edward Benlowes record Japan as 'Chipangu' or 'Nippon'.

[20] *the land of Gog and Magog:* a range of low hills on the borders of Essex and Cambridgeshire, for ever in tutelage to a pair of mythical giants.

[21] *Radwinter:* the second element is probably Old English *trēo*, 'tree'. If so, the first element is probably an unrecorded Old English woman's name, *Raēdwynn*. *(Oxford Dictionary of Place Names)*

[22] *the famous Elizabethan pastor's dwelling:* here William Harrison, rector at Radwinter, wrote his *Historical Description of the Iland of Britaine* in the 1570s.

[23] *the seashores of Bohemia:* a phrase sometimes quoted in evidence of Shakespeare's supposed ignorance of geography, but it is said that the otherwise landlocked country did in fact have littoral access to the Adriatic in Elizabethan times.

[24] *a husbandman, thirty years his senior:* the author's probable ancestor, William Cobb of Dorchester, Oxon., took part in a riot in 1554, a bad year to do so, with Bloody Mary on the throne.

[25] *Exodus:* 'If a man shall cause a field ... to be eaten, and shall put in his beast, and shall feed in another man's field; of the best of his own field ... shall he make restitution.' This is exactly how William Cobb fell foul of the law.

[26] *Hempstead. The highwayman Dick Turpin born here:* In 1705. A more worthy son of the village was William Harvey (1578-1657) who discovered the circulation of the blood. Of Dick Turpin *Dictionary of National Biography* says, 'a very commonplace ruffian who owes all his fame to the literary skill of Harrison Ainsworth, *Rookwood*, 1834.'

[27] *pair o' ankle-jacks:* the Essex labourer, used to wearing hobnail boots, applied this contemptuous term to shoes.

[28] *poets live and walk:* Dylan Thomas, *Portrait of the Artist as a Young Dog*.

[29] *the Bartlow Hills:* 'A public footpath through sycamore and ash saplings leads suddenly to four astonishing tumuli – the Bartlow Hills. They were part of some Romano-British headquarters, c. 100 AD. The mounds contained walled tombs. Grave goods of glass, decorated bronze and enamel.' (Norman Scarfe, *Essex – a Shell Guide,* 1975)

[30] *I decide to make my aim the sky:* a sad reflection on the decline of poetic sensibilities over 350 years, for Cyrano de Bergerac, faced with the need to walk on the surface of the sun, said he was 'ashamed to walk upon the daylight.'

[31] *I had all three:* scholars may think Coel's remarks confirm that the medieval *Laws of Wales* were based on a far older tradition.

[32] *a man with a very big nose:* Cyrano de Bergerac, whose *Voyage to the Moon* is quoted here, in the translation by John Aldington.

[33] *Better than going down in history:* according to *Brewer's Readers Handbook,* there were two legendary British kings with the name of 'Coïl': Coïl the First preceded Porrex, son of Gorboduc; Porrex was murdered by his mother for slaying his brother; Coïl the Second was the father of Lucius who, legend claims, was the first British king to embrace Christianity, in the late second century AD.

[34] Harold Bloom draws attention to this in *The Anxiety of Influence.* Haiku has a distinctive contribution to make, in that it affords an opportunity for all to contribute to that Great Poem, if only through appreciation.

first line maze

a bust of wet clay	under a blue sky
a blowfly unseen	under bamboo
a boil in the nose	under sandals
a boundless pleasure	unexpectedly
after gardening	under snowy pines
a diffuse smoke	under the Plough
after spring gales	under different trees
a crow's wings	up and down the lawn
after mating	walking on my own
after the birth	weekend in autumn
after the eclipse	we're here, love, again
after the tiff	we sit on a plane
after the hanging	we sweat on our bed
before the bonfire	when the red light shows
before the icon	where they groom the dead
before he washes	while the lesson's read
between dusk and dawn	whirling wind
between the legs of a cow	while he drills my teeth
birds burble	with fly-crammed beak
bin bags	within the shadow
blown off a cart	with a shared umbrella
blind man	with wind-sealed lips
brewing morning tea	wind through my shirt
bugger the deadline	with urgency
bulging cheeks	woman in a bar
bubble bath	wretched scarecrow

Note: A lot of previously published haiku bargained with me to be included and have edged their way in as a jumbled index of their first lines only. They may be read in a variety of directions – down one column and then down the other, hopping across from column to column from top to bottom, even diagonally, or from bottom to top.